Everything is a Gift

Jean-Jacques Trifault

EVERYTHING IS A GIFT
Jean-Jacques Trifault
Footsteps to Wisdom Publishing

Cover design by Kasia Krawczyk
For more information and for other speeches visit the website www.footstepstowisdom.org

Table of Contents

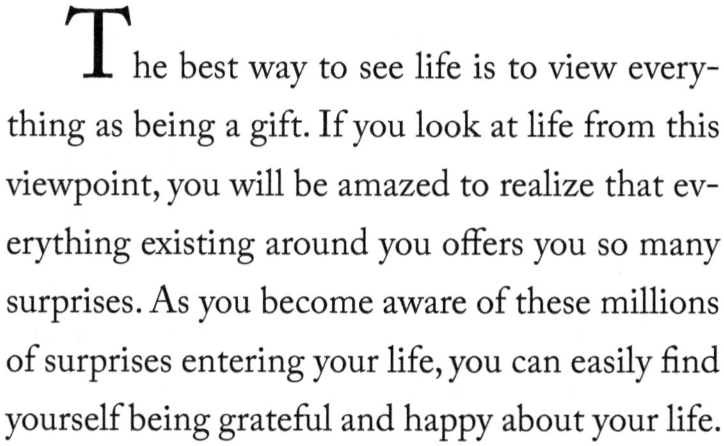

Everything is a Gift

The best way to see life is to view everything as being a gift. If you look at life from this viewpoint, you will be amazed to realize that everything existing around you offers you so many surprises. As you become aware of these millions of surprises entering your life, you can easily find yourself being grateful and happy about your life.

Being grateful will allow you to perceive everyone and everything around you in a very different way than you usually do. If you can step outside of your own skin and observe yourself from the eyes of a third person, you might notice that, like most people, you tend to think you never have enough. It is from this attitude of lacking and therefore needing to have more that you might develop the view – 'It is my right to have what I want because I deserve it' – and start to feel you should be given everything. Perhaps someone even taught you to think this way. However, if you cannot get what you consider is your right to have, you will become negative and find it impossible to be grateful or happy.

Another kind of thinking that you might observe within yourself is that everything and everyone must revolve around you. This viewpoint will block you from perceiving events occurring in your life as positive. Rather, you will perceive things as your enemy since they do not automatically revolve around you. You will not be able to welcome new events, new words or new people, and this will lead you to become antagonistic and to feel that the world is against you.

From where did you get the idea that everything must revolve around you? It is usually because you have a strong sense of self-value. You perceive yourselves as good people, and think it is therefore normal to receive good things. But because of this attitude, even though you may receive many good things, you don't feel the necessity to check whether you are grateful or not about what you receive.

Usually children like to receive things but do not like to show appreciation to their parents. If this attitude is projected onto a global scale, humankind looks very much like ungrateful children. But isn't it painful to have a child who is not grateful to you, the parent? Indeed then, it must be more painful to the One who created all of us. But since we do not know what God feels, we continue to carry the attitude that it is normal that we receive everything we want because we are good, because we think that if we were bad, we would not receive anything. We think this even though we somehow know that God is the giver of love, and that His love does not depend on what kind of person we are. And it is true, God continues to give because God cannot help giving. This is called, 'unconditional love'.

Giving and Receiving

One president, John F. Kennedy, said that what is important is not what your country gives to you, but what you can give to your country. This thought is close to the law of true love. What you can give is more important than what you can take. Yet we often reverse this phrase, thinking what we can take is the most important thing in life.

Since giving is so important, the question we need to ask ourselves is, what is giving? Giving starts from our mind, from thinking that everything is a gift. Most of us think everything is ours or that it should be ours. But instead of "should" be or "must" be, there is another way to see life. We can think that everything is a blessing or a miracle, that everything is a precious gift, offered to us by the hand of Life.

For example, if there is someone who cooks for you, you need to remember that the person is not obliged to do so, but it is a gift from him or her to you. Then you will find your mind and heart becoming grateful. If you look with the viewpoint that the person should cook for you, you will complain if you feel he or she cooks poorly or is late in serving the meal. Certainly, if the desire to give is foremost in your mind, you will always find the way to be grateful, instead of wanting to take, and then the thought you have toward the one who is cooking will be entirely different.

Indeed, I will say to you, only gratefulness toward life will grow your personality and give you happiness. So, if you find yourself complaining, it is because your attitude is to want something for yourself. Therefore the real difficulty for you is to maintain the attitude of never wanting anything for yourself. Interestingly, by not wanting anything, you will come to realize that you already have many things and are rich in ways that you could not have imagined. If you try to keep a heart of giving, you will eventually have the amazing privilege to discover the true nature of God, who gives because it is the way that He can continue to be the God of love.

How we receive things is also important. If we cannot learn to receive something as a gift, we will reject the miracle of it. This action of rejection will tragically remove the element of love that is contained within each gift, and therefore we will feel miserable because we will be unable to feel love even though it is there.

To receive the love of God, you must recognize what is given to you. If you want your soul to be filled up by love, you need to perceive each situation as a gift being given to you. And, if you can recognize what others do for you, this is also an action of loving God, because no human being does something for others if he was not educated by God or by his conscience to think to give. Even if someone does just one good action in the midst of many selfish actions, we should consider this one good action as being pure and give recognition to it. Yes, if a person says, 'Good morning' to you, you need to remember that he doesn't have to say anything to you, it is a gift, and therefore you will feel so thankful to this person.

God's Miracle Through People

However, your attitude usually is to want something without recognizing the miracle of it. You need to remember, you do not receive the blue sky because you are a good person or a bad person. The blue sky is a gift for everyone. The tragedy is you think you should receive things because you are good, and when you don't receive a blessing you think you are bad. Therefore the action of receiving becomes connected with good and evil. As long as you choose the viewpoint that you are good when you receive something and you are bad when you don't receive what you want, you cannot maintain your happiness. Your attitude should be, you are grateful when you receive something. And, if you don't receive anything it is not because you are bad, but perhaps it is just because the people around you do not know they should give something to others, or maybe they did give something to somebody else, just not to you yet.

Your tendency may be to blame not just the person but eventually to blame God when you don't receive something you want. But remember, God cannot force people to give, even though He may want to give something to you. God wants to give many things, but often He does not have anyone whom He can use to perform this kind of miracle. God wants to be everywhere to give, but He does not have enough people with the same desire to give, therefore He cannot do it. Because there are so few people who want to follow the principle of God's love, you may receive only a little, and you may find yourself accusing God, thinking He doesn't love you.

Unfortunately, the tendency of human beings is if they don't receive according to their desire, they will have no compassion toward God's situation, but instead will freely accuse Him for not giving them what they want.

On the other hand, when you do receive

something, I don't think you receive it with the viewpoint it can be God giving to you through the person, do you? Therefore, you cannot receive love in that situation either, because you don't recognize it as a gift from God.

When I look at the situation of God, sometimes He may have someone pure enough to pass through to give you something, but in another instance He doesn't have anyone. That is the sorrowful part of God and the sorrowful part of His children. Yes, indeed, human beings cry because they need a physical sign to know that God loves them. And Heavenly Father cries because He cannot find anyone pure enough on this planet to pass through to give His love.

To remedy this sad situation, please start to recognize everything as a gift, because everything comes from goodness. If someone opens the door for you, you should not think it is because he should do that. Remember, the person did something good because there was some goodness inside him. I believe you do notice the difference if someone forgets to hold the door open in front of you, and it smashes your nose. So, if someone holds the door open, can you accept it was God through the person's goodness doing so?

Have no Expectations

Your perception will determine your destiny. Don't say that someone "should" hold the door open. Say, "Thank you for holding the door for me so that I can pass through." Then you can feel God's love through that person and God's love for that person.

Therefore, it is best to have no expectations. You will find that complaining thoughts come when you want someone to do something for you, and this someone cannot fulfill your wish. You might be surprised to see yourself getting angry if you do not receive what you expect. Instead of that, when you don't receive something you want, it is better to say to yourself it is okay because the person has the right to freely give or not give, and is not obliged to give to you.

If you want to be happy on this planet Earth, you need to have the viewpoint that everything comes to you as a gift, because only with this viewpoint will you be able to create peace within yourself. It is this peace that will allow you to perceive the love of God through the people around you. With this attitude of recognizing everything is a gift, you will be able to live well with others, by removing the potential for complaint against others. To have peace inside of yourself, it is incredibly important to expect nothing from others, and instead to carry the viewpoint of God, the Origin of love, which is that everyone around you is a gift coming to you.

If every person lives according to this viewpoint, life becomes simple and harmonious, and surely people will feel welcomed by one another. And, since everyone wants to give more often to you, and you also want to give to others, then the peace you have within yourself will turn into happiness.

To maintain this viewpoint that everything is a gift, you need to remember that God is the Origin of love, and therefore, the origin of every gift. When you remember this thought, God can give love to you and through you. If you train yourself to think this way, you will receive so much love, which I think you will be happy to have. But if you don't want to act upon this viewpoint or if you reject God as the origin, you will neither receive love nor find peace in your mind and soul. In this, you can understand that your destiny depends on whether your mind has this viewpoint or not.

Peace Inside Yourself

If we can understand the attributes of love and how to see life, we will find we can receive as much love as we want. We will realize that our physical life exists with a purpose. However, without knowing the purpose, we cannot see the full picture of what exists around us and the value it contains.

The person who says that everything he receives originates in some way from God will be able to receive love. This is also true concerning how a child views his parents. If a child believes that his parents represent God to some degree, that child will be able to feel love from his parents. However, if the child is not taught to make the connection between his or her parents and

God, this child will no longer feel love from his or her parents, because the line to the source of life is cut off. Only by being taught the viewpoint that some characteristics of God are indeed manifesting in his or her parents, will this child receive the elements of goodness that will allow him or her to grow into a beautiful being.

We should never forget the importance of expressing gratitude for what is around us. For example, if we can recall an earlier time when people first sailed from Europe to America, they said 'Thank You' to God to be alive, even though the journey was hard and many died during the first winter in this new land. During this long winter they were starving but they did not want to use the seeds they had saved for the spring planting. Those persons who accepted to not touch the seeds must have been grateful to God so many times in order to be capable of controlling their physical needs. And I do think, for them to choose to be grateful to God, they must have learned to see everything around them as being a gift from God, and not to take anything for granted.

How about you? What kind of faith or what thought would you have if you were in the same kind of situation? Would you consider that everything you experience really is a gift coming from God to you?

The most important thing for our life is to pass through every daily life situation with the right viewpoint. So I can say, to live well with others, we need to remove any expectation that can provoke us to become negative. If we consider we want to have many friends and a beautiful family, we need to acquire a grateful mind, expecting nothing from others but seeing everything as coming from God as the origin of love. Indeed, this viewpoint will make our soul peaceful and pleasant for others to live with.

The Living Gift

Do you consider you have the right to question what your friend gives to you? Or do you have the right to take responsibility to receive any gift with the best viewpoint you can find? Your choice and your viewpoint will depend on how highly you value what lives around you. Surely it is in your best interest to gain the viewpoint that will allow you to receive the most love.

Alas, most of you reject the value of your friend because you forget that he or she comes from God. But the most tragic event of all is to not see your husband or wife as the representative of God, since this lack of thought will make it impossible to receive love through each other. From now on, you need to acknowledge that what your brother, sister, friend or spouse gives to you is also initiated from God.

Interestingly, many of you who do not usually acknowledge God will suddenly ask Him to help you when you are passing through some hard situation, or you will curse Him for the difficulty. For some reason you connect negative events to God, but not the positive ones, which is difficult to comprehend, if you are trying to be impartial. I think it is not fair to identify every negative event as being connected to God, considering that life is not only composed of problems but also of joyful and positive events.

So the question can arise, why do human beings not recognize God equally through different events? Why does it seem to be unpopular to connect God with anything positive? Perhaps people choose that viewpoint because they have an interest in accusing God. But surely the effect of this tendency to associate only negative events with God will be to not allow you to receive the love that is there.

It is also good to recognize that there are different levels of gifts. The simplest one is something you can buy with money. The next level is the gift of knowledge. Actually, people often feel it is normal to receive knowledge because it is intangible. The third level of gift is a living being. This gift is very precious and sensitive, and therefore the quality you need in order to keep this kind of gift in your life requires a high viewpoint that can encourage you to value the gift over and over again.

Treasure Chest of Love

Perhaps you did receive this kind of gift, like having a friend. In the beginning, you may have taken the view that this friend was a gift from God, but soon found that to maintain this viewpoint demanded a great deal of effort. Most people believe that a human being is created as a lovely treasure, and in our hearts we believe that friendship and marriage are high gifts; however we don't acknowledge that God was the first one who valued human beings as the place where harmonious love can sustain itself. Then it becomes difficult for us to continue to value each other.

The important thing is, can you appreciate this living person as a gift for as long as your life endures? The only way you can do that is by perceiving this living gift as coming from God. If you can see that way, your heart can become like God's heart in the flesh through this process.

This is the reason you need to be careful with your thoughts. In case you lose the value or the viewpoint that this person is a gift, you need to recall the time when you were alone. Through this, you can rediscover the original reason why you chose to look for a friend or to marry someone, which was to not be alone. But because you do not know how to keep this thought that permits you to recognize the value of your gift, you start to complain about him or her, and your heart can become hard to the point you can no longer see anything good about this person.

Because human beings do not know the value of keeping God's viewpoint, they most of the time see themselves as victims and because of that, they choose to complain about others, hoping to remove the pain. But the truth is, the more their complaint increases, the more their ability to view everything around them as a gift leaves them, to the point that what they used to see as a gift becomes an enemy to them.

Therefore, you need to be able to consistently maintain the view that your friends are gifts to you, before you even consider looking for a spouse. If you cannot be grateful for your friends, who you only meet some of the time, you will not be able to live with one person throughout your whole life without attacking this gift.

From this viewpoint you can see how difficult it is to live as husband, wife and children together. But if you can keep the viewpoint that every person is a gift from God, then you will never make the mistake of attacking or breaking your gift. The longer you can think this way, the longer the time you can keep your relationships in good shape, which is surely valuable. But the most important benefit you can receive from keeping this viewpoint is the love that God can give to you, throughout your entire life.

Meeting the Son of God

If you could see life from the viewpoint of the One who gives the gifts, you would realize how difficult it is to create a holy or true human being. But regardless of the effort invested in this majestic work, God gave to the people His True Son, knowing that when His Son was in the midst of them, they would act based on whatever viewpoint they had. Therefore, if gratefulness is not the viewpoint you take in your life, maybe you would act the same way as the people did when they saw the Son of God, rejecting him, if you also could have the chance to meet him.

What was the reason 2000 years ago for such a dramatic, tragic situation to occur, when Jesus was the most precious gift God wanted to give to mankind? The reason is, when you do not learn to see everything as a gift every day, you amputate your senses. Without your senses, you cannot perceive whatever or whoever is in front of you, even the most holy person or event. Therefore, as wisdom, it is preferable to always take care to see people as gifts from God. Then you will not make a mistake if you meet a holy person or a Son of God in disguise.

For you to become beautiful, you need to see life as a gift every day and be very careful to not break any friendships, which are like rare and precious flowers in your garden. Many people can come to your life, but please consider each one as a gift from God. If you do so you will be able to grow God's heart in yourself.

This physical world is the place where gifts are created. From all of these gifts, people are the highest. The most wonderful reason for people to be on this planet is so they can create beauty in themselves and become a gift for those around them. Perhaps in your life you have met many good people and because of them you want to become good as well. When you try to grow goodness in yourself and start to educate yourself to see every human as a gift, you will realize it takes so much time to create a beautiful person.

Conversely, if you for some reason desire to create ugliness, you have only to lose respect for the gifts in life, and you will find yourself attacking everything around you and judging the people you used to value. Eventually, with age on your shoulders, you will judge yourself for what you have done to others.

Creating Goodness Takes Time

So when you look at a beautiful person, remember how long it took for God and for that person to create in him or herself a beautiful personality. Don't believe he or she became like that just by accident. Remember, each person comes from at least several years of cultivating good thoughts and actions in order to become a good person. Since it takes great effort to create what is considered to be a good person, then how much longer will it take to create a truly beautiful person? Therefore, we need to be so careful with the gifts we receive. We need to think, "What merit do I have to be able to receive any gift in the first place?" – knowing that sometimes we are not as good as the person we see.

If you can keep this humble attitude, you will surely be able to take care of every gift God gives to you, regardless sometimes it looks like a gift is coming into your life for just a short time. If you dream perhaps someday of being married to someone for eternity, you will need to keep a humble and grateful attitude because you know this gift was created from a deep part of the heart of the giver, and eventually from God. Then I know you will be a happy person for all your life and you can enjoy to be with someone for eternity.

But if you start to choose a belief that the person who lives with you is doing things you consider to be normal or to be expected, you will start to find the meaning of the word frustration, especially if this person does not fulfill all of your expectations. And this frustration will transform into negativity, until eventually you will reject your spouse or whoever is next to you, if not physically, then at least mentally, and most importantly, heartistically.

If you make a mistake in how you view the person that God brought into your life, what will God feel about you? Because it is very difficult to keep considering a human as a gift for all your life, it might be wise therefore to learn to be friends with animals first. When you feel stable in keeping your respect for animals, you can start a short-term friendship with a human being, and then a longer-term friendship, hoping to keep the view that your friend is a gift. Eventually, based on your success, you can be qualified to receive a spouse as an eternal gift.

The Taste of Heaven

Did you experience to say sometimes that you

wanted to love God? If so, surely God will say that loving Him means loving people with all your heart, soul and flesh. If you can be very careful to keep your attitude toward them as living gifts, then you will also become the gift of God for the people who will have the honor to be with you.

Now you know what makes you mature: it is the way you respect each category of gift you receive. As stated before, the first category is material things, like toys or a car or a house. The second category is knowledge, or the word of God. If you respect these two categories of gifts, you will arrive to the place where you have the desire to meet people and make friends with them, to the point you will want to create a home with someone, who is the third category of gift.

Based on the category of the third gift, you

will surely want a person who will be your gift for eternity and for whom you can be their gift for eternity. The reason you will want this is so that you can receive heavenly love, which we can characterize as the highest gift or the fourth category, in order that you can begin to taste the love of Heaven.

To achieve this high vision, you have to constantly focus on what your mind is thinking, in order to maintain the thought that everything is a gift. In trying to achieve this thought, you will need to remove your old way of thinking that things must come to you because you believe you deserve them. If you have a friend and you want to keep your friendship for a long time, you have to learn to keep the thought that whenever this person gives you something it is because he wants to do so, and not because he must do so based on your friendship. Whatever he does has to be perceived from your viewpoint as a gift. If you are no longer able to recognize your friend's action as a gift, you will come to a place where you feel nothing from his action, or from any action by people who pass through your life. Because of this, you will always feel that your friend, and others, do not love you.

Perception Determines Destiny

How many people have offered you lunch or dinner throughout your life? As well, how many people still give you something each day, small or big, like a kind word or a compliment? The point is, how do you perceive what they give to you? Surely, you must have experienced many gifts coming to you each day, each week, each month and each year, and therefore you should feel so much love, isn't that right? But perhaps you don't feel any love. Instead, maybe you feel isolated. How is this possible?

Personally, I did observe this situation, and I

concluded it is not what people give to you that makes you feel happy, it is the way you perceive what they give to you that makes you feel happiness. This explains why, if you do not connect what you receive with the viewpoint that God wants to give to you, you will start to feel empty and dry. Due to this emotional starvation, you will find yourself opposing more and more the things that you used to hold dear, to the point you will eventually turn against the people in your life, as well as the One who created you.

We often hear people remarking that they did not feel love from their parents when they were children, which is the same tendency that people have toward God. But if you have the opportunity to question those specific parents, they will say they gave everything they had to their children, especially love.

And they will not understand why their children have some criticism toward them. Of course we can investigate the motivation of the parents, to see if what they did for their children was actually based on love or on something else. But the best way to end this feeling of lack of love is to take responsibility for not having learned to see everything you receive as a gift. You will therefore realize that it is logical that you did not feel love from your parents when you were a child, or feel love from God, who was aware of your situation, because you were not seeing everything as a gift.

If we retrace the past, we can hear every generation telling the same story: their parents never loved them enough. We are perhaps perceiving the emotions of our ancestors who maybe still cry about not having received love, to the point they continue to accuse others. You may even hear these accusations sometimes in your own mind, believing that it is you who does not have love. But I can tell you, there is a way to stop these internal accusations that have been passed down from generation to generation. You just need to ask yourself, did you reject your parents for not giving you enough of what is usually called love? Or did you reject them because you did not learn the thought that would permit you to see their actions as actions of love, the thought that everything is a gift?

See With Both Eyes

At the moment when your family or friends are giving something to you, if you see what they give as only a physical object, it is like seeing with only one eye, the eye that has the responsibility to acknowledge physical actions or objects. But if you do not develop your other eye, which has the responsibility to see the purpose behind the actions, you will be blind and unable to recognize that all those actions are gifts for you. Therefore, if you are content to see life only from the eye that perceives the material side, you are condemned to never receive true love. On the other hand, if you learn to educate your second eye, which is created to see the internal purpose for which things are given to you, then you will have the whole vision that will help you to see everything in the right form, proportion and volume. And through this dual vision, you will be able to sense the love that is contained in everything that is given to you.

Did you often experience that people greet you, saying "How do you do?" When we hear these words, the question we should ask ourselves is, who is asking? The first view will be, it is indeed that specific person. From the other eye (or the other ear) we should perceive it is God who is asking us through the person. If we can train our consciousness to be alert to this new viewpoint, then at the same speed as the event is taking place, we will be aware that we are not alone, because we will feel God's presence with us in that very same moment.

Now, if you are the one who gives the greeting, "How are you doing this morning?" to your friend or to your spouse, I suggest to you, please think it is God who wants to give that greeting. If you can think this way, while speaking the words of greeting, you will feel a lot of emotion coming to you for those people, who perhaps are not even aware of your motivation for greeting them in the morning.

In another situation, if you serve someone and think it is God who is serving through you, you will receive love at the same moment you are serving that person. Therefore you will not feel empty at the end of your life, but instead you will feel content with the maturity you have gained through the process of giving and receiving God's love.

Unification of Spirit and Matter

Now you can understand that you must reunite what was separated in you or was not developed in you. Since you were only educated based on a materialistic viewpoint, you could not feel love from anything besides what material things could produce in your physical senses. When you accept to learn to have the proper thought, symbolizing your spiritual mind, toward an object you receive, symbolizing your material aspect, you will become capable of reunifying your two parts into one self.

In other words, if you fill your mind with the consciousness of the presence of God who is living all around you, this consciousness will help you to remove the thought that everything you receive is just matter and that you should have it because you deserve it. Through removing this materialistic thought, you will discover that everything you received was given by free will, originating from the free will of God. Then you will be able to receive well, and what you receive will become substantial love inside your heart.

Who cooks for you every night? Is it God? Or is it just your spouse or your friend? Some of you will maybe reject the internal view, and if you do so this means that you reject the most honorable reason your spouse or your friend gives you something, and the memory you retain will be only of his or her secular action.

If you view things in a humanistic way, you will not see God giving to you through another person; instead you will just say it was a good action or even a self-promoting action. In other words, you will separate good actions from their origin in God. And when you separate everything inside your mind, you remove the potential to feel love.

But if there are some people who only recognize the secular form of the action and therefore miss out on receiving the love that is within it, there are others who reject the material aspect of what happens around their lives, in the name of wanting to protect what they believe God to be, and they also miss out on love. These people have the tendency to believe it is God acting alone who gives them everything they receive, without recognizing the love in the person who gave to them.

But, as a matter of fact, by not recognizing the person's action, it is like they eliminate one of their eyes. They prefer to blind one eye in order to say that it was God who cooked for them, but never the person who was in the kitchen. Maybe this occurs because they consider this person as not having the same value as God. But to receive love we need to recognize both God and the person who initiates the gift as having equal value. If we deny one side based on whatever belief we may have, we cannot perceive the love that is there.

Due to this reality of people protecting the aspect of sight which they value, one group will recognize the spiritual side and work hard to deny the secular side, in the hope of identifying themselves as internal and spiritual people; the other group will have the tendency to reject the viewpoint that God is behind all matter, in the name of claiming themselves to be protectors of the physical reality. Both groups choose their devotion and blind one eye in the name of increasing the sight in the eye they prefer, without knowing that this destroys the base upon which they could have received love from God.

What I am trying to explain here is that you should recognize fully what exists around you in order to receive the love that is there but not yet perceivable until you make this step. You must acquire these two viewpoints to be able to become a harmonious being who can receive love. From now on, if you recognize that the internal viewpoint and the physical action are equally important, you will perceive love coming inside of your whole being, making your mind and your body unite. This unity will help you to develop a beautiful personality, which is the result of a positive mind and a humble body.

Keep God's Viewpoint

These two viewpoints will allow you to see that even if it is your enemy who smiles to you, even for just one second, you need to accept that it was God who smiled to you. In some situations, you might realize that a person has just one beautiful aspect. But even here, can you accept that it is okay for someone not to be completely beautiful, because at least this situation obliges you to create a beautiful mind? In other words, you can discover whether you are able keep God's viewpoint in your mind and whether you are able to love God, by loving all kinds of people.

Perhaps we can recall Jesus' words asking if we saw him in the person sitting next to us, smiling at us, or even frowning at us. Jesus said he was there next to us but we did not see him, he was speaking to us and we didn't hear him, he needed clothes and we didn't clothe him.

Indeed, these words challenge us deeply. No matter where we come from we need to admit, indeed, we all made the same mistake; we forgot to see him through others. The reason it is possible to make this error is because we do not see from the viewpoint of everything being a gift, or that everything is given from God or from Jesus.

What will determine if you can see everything as a gift? If you reject the belief that God is the Creator of this universe, you will be unable to accept the internal viewpoint that everything is a gift, because if no one created this universe, then there can be no one who is in a position to offer it as a gift to you. This will make it impossible for you to be aware that all kinds of big or small actions are the gifts of God's love for you. But if you do accept this higher viewpoint, you will accept to value God as the Giver through the generosity of people, instead of thinking whatever they give is supposed to happen or must happen.

This can be applied to many situations. How about the money you earn? Is it God's gift to you? Or is it just your money because you worked hard for it? If you claim that everything you receive belongs to you, or that everything comes just from your personal efforts, you will still be able to obtain physical objects. But very soon someone will make a remark or you will hear inside yourself that you are selfish, and hearing these words will surely not give you any pleasure.

So, regardless you try by many means to not hear these unpleasant words, the fact is, you cannot really escape from them, unless you change your view toward what you receive, in this case accepting the money as a gift from God to you. Then you will no longer hear you are selfish. Instead, you will begin to receive love from God, and you will hear people tell you that you are a very nice person.

Create Your Destiny

We all desire to be considered loving people, but we need to receive love in order to give love. Now you know that to receive love you must recognize every event as a gift that is originally given from God through people. If, at the moment you receive some material thing, you say it was God who gave it to you, then by consistently saying this you will become a lovely person and will have love to give to others.

Your destiny on this Earth is to keep this viewpoint, in order to feel God is living next to you. If you can do so, you will no longer feel a lack of love. But to accept this viewpoint that every gift originates from God, you need first to humble yourself and acknowledge that you did not create the universe, and accept to educate your mind to believe everything coming to you is a gift. If you adopt this thought as part of your life, you will surely lose your discontentment.

By recognizing the universe as the creation of God and not of yourself, you will also be able to see that every little event in your life is promoted by God through the goodness of human beings, and this will create happiness in you. The more you recognize God as the cause, the more love will come inside you, as the effect. But if you deny the invisible cause, you will remove the invisible love as well.

You should be aware that the thought or the viewpoint you choose will create yourself differently. You are responsible for your destiny, since you are capable of thinking and freely choosing whatever thought you want to have,

You must have realized by now that a thought is not just an intellectual concept you encounter when you are reading a book, but a thought is made to be used when you interact with others, for example someone who is cooking for you, or doing your laundry. If you can look at the situation and simultaneously remember that it is God through the person who is doing something, then I will say, you are making the perfect base for the love of God to come to you in that moment. This moment of fusion is the one you need to make again and again.

Become a Beautiful Gift

In your lifetime, even if you do nothing extraordinary to change the destiny of this world, it will be a miracle in the modern sense for you to take responsibility to look at people with this most beautiful viewpoint. If you receive a material gift and acknowledge the person's gift from an internal viewpoint, you will be building your beauty, and surely many people will feel happy to see you. If others are also educated with this thought of believing everything is a gift, they will also appreciate you much more, to the point they will be confused about whether it is you as a human they see, or if it is God they see, through you.

So, if you really analyze my viewpoint, you will realize nothing in the physical world can make someone happy until he or she becomes a beautiful human being through the process of recognizing the goodness in others. The reason this view is so important is because we know to some degree that every human being wishes to be recognized as the child of God, not just as the child of his or her father and mother. And, regardless of what a person accomplishes secularly, surely everyone wishes for someone to recognize the goodness inside of his or her soul.

To achieve this recognition, you will need to magnetically attract Heaven by your thought, so Heaven can be with you when you look at someone, or give or receive something. For that, you will need to ask to have God's eyes, God's ears, God's heart. With these new senses, you will more easily accept others, because you will think it is God who is looking at you, speaking to you, listening to you, through the other person.

So I repeat, in order to love others you just need to remember that everything is a gift from God. If someone gives you something, it is no longer what 'should' happen to you; instead you need to look at what is being given to you as a miracle of love, regardless every event is physical.

Please, practice this exercise in your mind and in your flesh every day of your life. Then you will be so grateful to have someone to talk to, or even for someone who gives you a hard time, because you will have the viewpoint that you can grow your love. To love someone means you maintain the view that permits you to give and receive the love of God to and from any person. This is the reason Jesus Christ said that when you give something to the poor you give to him, and when you smile to someone you smile to him. Then, even if the person doesn't smile back it doesn't matter because you wanted to smile to

God anyway.

In conclusion, you need to understand that Heaven is waiting for you. The more you see life around you as the living creation of God, the more you will be the beautiful person Heaven wants and needs. Unless you choose this road every day, you are actually taking the deviant road and you will be pulled backward little by little.

So please be humble and accept to learn. If you do so, all the love of Heaven will belong to you and then you will be able to build a kingdom which Heaven wishes to be part of.

Thank you to learn, so you can become holy and have love.

How Gratefulness Creates a Beautiful Heart

On this day I want to speak to you about the value of gratefulness as seen from its effect upon human beings' heart, mind, and body. Gratefulness is an attitude toward life. When you decide to be grateful, it means you are learning to recognize what is good around and also inside of yourself. Recognizing goodness is the main component of learning how to experience love. When you have difficulty recognizing goodness, or recognizing what people give to you, you actually are rejecting love. For love to function, you must recognize mentally and verbally what somebody gives to you by expressing thanks.

Through this process, you are both receiving the love inside you, and you are giving back love to the giver. It is very important to complete the full circle of love by saying thank you, because it stimulates the subject, the person who initiates. When you respond to a giver, this person can feel joy inside himself, and this will stimulate the giver, or the subject, to continue to offer something to you, the object, through which you can also experience joy.

The reality is, however, that human beings usually complain more often than they are grateful. Consciously or unconsciously, many people use complaint as a way to relate with others or to assert their superiority. But if they could see what was happening inside their soul, they would discover that the more they reject what other people give to them, the more they reject the most fundamental part of life, which is love. When you complain about the events or the people around your life, you are actually rejecting love. Love is an element of energy that exists inside the objects around you, which you need in order for your soul to grow and function. When you complain, you are stunting the growth of your original soul, as well everything that is supposed to flourish around it.

Let me explain this in more depth. I believe you have studied that all the creation around you is composed of energy and matter. When these two aspects interact with each other, they start to augment or to recreate each other. I will take a healthy cell as an example. On the material side, more molecules or particles are ingested, and on the energy side, more energy is being created. But if either the material side or the energy starts to decrease, the cell will die sooner or later.

Human beings also consist of both aspects of energy and matter. When you have an attitude of gratitude, you are augmenting your energy side, which will transfer the love energy it receives into your matter, or your particles. This is why you can see the importance of responding to love. The rotation between your matter and the energy of love will develop your soul or spirit as long as the two are functioning harmoniously.

Mysterious Human Beings

Therefore the important question is, how are you going to promote the harmony necessary to ensure that love comes inside your being in order for you to develop your spirit? One obstacle I observe in human beings is that most people do not recognize what comes into their lives. Most do not see what people give to them as the miracle of the day. Even more, we usually do not perceive that it is God who permits those miracles to happen. Most people are blind to what happens around them.

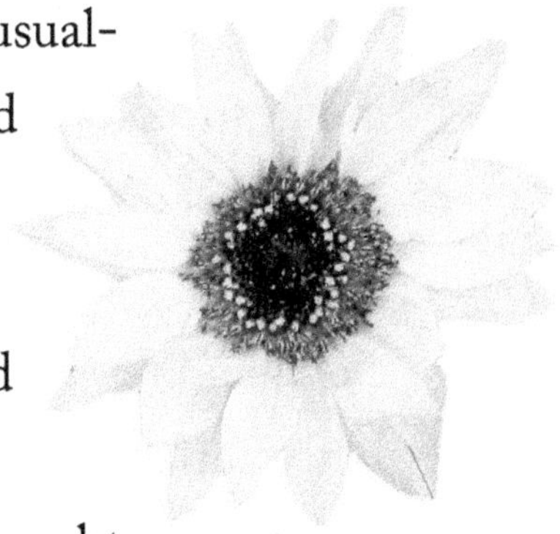

For example, when you bought your newspaper this morning, did you hear the greeting of the one who sold you the paper? Or, if he did not greet you, perhaps he smiled. Unless you hear or see what is around you, you cannot receive the love that is the internal element of each object of life. If you are blind to what people around you give, you cannot recognize each miracle and therefore you cannot receive love for your soul.

I believe that human beings are the most beautiful thing existing in this world, because they are mysterious in many ways, always changing the way they do things. If you do not learn to be grateful about these creatures that share so much in common with you, I believe you will develop a deep rejection against them with your complaints, to the point you will want to live alone and far away from them. If you find yourself wanting to be isolated, it means you can no longer find reasons to be grateful about others. But the biggest drama is that you will reject all the love that is mysteriously printed inside of every human action, and you will therefore stifle your soul.

The lesson to discover here is the more you learn to be grateful about what is around you, the more you receive love. This love you receive through everything is actually a part of God. It is like you are absorbing God. More exactly, an attitude of gratefulness is like eating food particles that your soul can ingest. In other words, every time you are grateful you are ingesting God's love.

The more you are aware of what you see and are grateful about what is happening around your life, the more your soul will breathe love, which is a vital element for its development. If you can only be grateful about five percent of your life, it means that you only receive five percent of what God wants you to receive. On the other hand, if you learn to be grateful about one hundred percent of your life, then you will indeed receive one hundred percent of God's love.

If you look at human beings from the aspect of love, you will realize the more a person is full of love, the more he or she is considered to be a good person. To be a bad person means to carry a small amount of love inside oneself. If the love inside is insignificant, you start to identify that person with a distasteful flavor that makes you repel him. As a result of that reality, the word 'bad' will begin to be associated with that person.

Breathing the Air of Love

Therefore the question is, how can you receive this love that you cannot see but can feel around you and within people? First of all, you can be grateful that you are endowed with the ability to capture love energy and multiply this love energy with other human beings. You can thank the Inventor for this incredible being that you are.

I believe the Being who created us must have had some reason to create us as such potentially lovely beings, instead of just creating us as beings with instinct only, which we find in the midst of the animal kingdom. The only possible reason I can think He did create us so majestically is because this Inventor must be made of love elements, and He wants us to have similar elements as He does, and be able to breathe the same air as He does, which is love air.

But if today human beings have lost their grateful minds, then it is not possible for God's love to be received by the human heart. In this case, we cannot achieve the same elements as God, or breathe the same air of love. As you all know, if the planet Earth were to lose its atmosphere it would not be able to sustain its beautiful array of life, which we testify about every day when we look through the window and see the leaves still attached to the trees or the grass still standing up straight. And surely, the greatest testimony to the miracle of the Earth's layer of atmosphere, which allows everything existing to reach its physical maturity, is the miracle of human life.

Similarly, a specific atmosphere is also necessary for our spiritual lives. For our soul to fulfill its destiny, which is to be God's child, it needs an atmosphere of love. If you understand my point, you will realize that the more you are grateful about your life, the more you will receive that love that is the invisible aspect of each object and each event. But if you complain, you reject the love inside each action, and you will finish your life on this planet Earth without having created an atmosphere of love for your soul to breathe and to grow to fruition with.

Can You Capture Love?

Therefore you need to ask yourself, how you are going to remove the quantity of complaint you express every day toward what you see? As well, how are you going to increase your quantity of gratefulness toward what is around you, in order to receive the invisible love of God?

To begin with, if you observe yourself, you will realize that there are two actions within love, the action of giving and the action of receiving. The action of giving love is usually something physical and the action of receiving love is responding with words of gratefulness. To illustrate this, I can say that the sun rising every morning is a physical event. Therefore, if we think the sun is rising for our sake, giving us light and warmth, we can easily be grateful about the sun and complete the cycle of giving and receiving, by saying "thanks".

Gratefulness makes a lot of difference for the relationship between the giver and the receiver. Yet, when I observe human behavior, I realize the most difficult thing to do is to be grateful about each gift we receive. One example is a mother who creates meals with variety and tastiness every day, but how many members of the family are grateful about her creations? It almost seems that to be grateful toward the mother is harder to do than to create the meal. Due to the lack of response, the love that was circulated in the process of the mother creating the meal cannot continue its journey. Because the members of the family do not say thank you for that specific event, love is unable to penetrate them. And because they do not receive love, this family will have a high possibility of finding themselves choosing the opposite of gratefulness, which is complaint.

If I were to show you the situation of your life, you would be amazed to realize how many objects and events you are not grateful about. Your life is full of millions of gifts to you, but if you do not learn to have a mind of gratefulness, it is as if you do not receive anything.

Therefore I hope, if your friend or your spouse creates something for you, you can humble yourself, accept it, and remember to express gratefulness. I hope you will remember that gratefulness is the way to give back love to the giver. Through this full circulation of love you will remove the frustration of the one who was giving without being recognized. And, if he or she accepts your compliment or words of gratefulness, this person will find a deeper level of joy, as will you.

The Third Dimension

This is the secret of experiencing another dimension, the third dimension of your being. What is the third dimension? To illustrate, let us look at a specific invention, the development of motion pictures, which began in the late 1800s. After a few decades, we found a way to match the images on the screen with sound, which was like adding a second dimension. The combination of these two created the movies we have today. However, there is another step in the process, which is to create a three dimensional movie, or a hologram.

Learning to be grateful can be compared to creating a three dimensional movie, because through gratitude you are developing a new dimension in yourself, your third dimension, the dimension of love. If you forget to be grateful, it is like making a movie without sound, which I do not consider very desirable to be watched. The moment you think gratefully in the midst of what you see, it is like adding sound to your film. It is still a flat or two dimensional movie, but much more appreciable than a silent film. Finally, if you verbalize your gratitude, it is like creating a hologram. The love energy that is in the midst of life can pass through this circular movement, making your heart expand and creating the third dimension.

The question now is, are you excited and responsive about life? Most of you believe that life is just material or instinctual, without considering the spiritual dimension that gratitude creates. But today, even many scientists accept that living beings not only have instincts but also have purpose inside their molecules. You as a human being are not just made of matter, but you also have the desire to be happy and to become beautiful. What you have not known about yourself is that you are made as a love being with the potential to become a citizen of the third dimension while living on this planet, allowing the people around you to enjoy being next to you.

How can you create the third dimension? I believe you have heard many philosophers and religious leaders telling you that you need to do good actions and have a positive mind in order to be happy, which is absolutely true. Yet to have that positive mind, you need to have a key thought. That key thought is an attitude of gratitude toward all things. Only through this thought can you keep a positive mind and receive the love needed in order to develop a lovely personality.

To make a point concerning our relationship with our Creator, I will say that the action of giving or initiating is important because it helps us discover the position of the Creator, who is always giving. But just as important is being able to receive love well, so the full circle of love can go back to the Creator. To do so you need to learn to be grateful for every event, which will help you to become a true object or receiver. True love can be received only when the positions of initiator and receiver are in harmony. The moment you respond well, the love you have received can expand, and this vibration of love can create excitement in you and in the ones with you.

So, do you want to be a flat or an exciting person? This is similar to asking if you want to see a silent or a talking or a three-dimensional movie. If all human beings become grateful today, we will become exciting people, and the happiness we are trying to find will not just be a dream but a reality. Regardless life was flat due to the impossibility of finding love, if you begin today to be grateful, all negative energy around you will disappear and will instead become positive energy. This will begin to create you into a three-dimensional being.

Love Energy Conception

Then if one day this three-dimensional being decides to become a parent, he or she will be capable of nourishing a new being, right from the stage of conception. This positive energy, which we call true love, will be the main factor of influence on the fetus, even above the physical characteristics of the parents. Because of this love, the fetus will surely start life very differently than if it were conceived without any drop of this love. A child who is conceived with the real energy of love will develop his or her senses differently, allowing this child to discover a higher level of potential.

The first stage of development in a child after the physical body is the growth of the mind, which blossoms due to receiving this love. This love has the attribute of being even more invisible than the world of the mind, however, and is in the position of an axis, allowing the mind to create a system of thought containing a positive nature. The more a child's mind can receive this love, the more you will see the development of positive thought taking place, which is more visible than love. The more this love is established, the more this child can identify him or herself as becoming mature and moving toward absolute goodness.

To illustrate this point, I will use the example of a bud. When you first see a bud it is hard to imagine what will come out from it. The development of the bud depends on receiving enough water, minerals, and light. If it receives these three elements consistently, you will start to see a flower blooming and there will be a fruit in the end.

Likewise, if you examine your mind in the way you examine a bud, you will realize there are different stages: the stage of the mind of a child, the stage of the mind of a young adult, and eventually the stage of the adult mind. Looking more closely, we can see several other stages, for example, the stage of a baby, of an adolescent, and of a grandparent's mind.

In order for each stage of mind to be correctly nourished and to mature, love is a necessity. If you cannot receive this love, it means you cannot mature your mind according to the corresponding age of your body, to the point you will feel your body's physical development surpasses the development of your mind. In other words, you will feel your mind stays at the stage of a child while your body is growing to resemble an adult or a parent. However, regardless what stage your mind attains, your body will eventually arrive to the stage of a grandparent due to the laws of biology. But it is rare to see somebody who looks externally like a grandparent also having the maturity of mind and love of a grandparent. Therefore, it means the mind does not evolve through the same system of nourishment as the body. This gap is more perceivable in people who have attained a more advanced age.

It is interesting that we usually have certain concepts about love. Where does our concept of love originate from? In the midst of your education, you may have learned that God is love, and due to that you became aware of the existence of love. As well, for some reason you probably believed that this love would come in your midst and be shared between you and your family and friends, and eventually with your spouse and children. Due to this belief, you measured the value of your relationships through the amount of love passing between each other.

However, I think it is quite sad to see people measuring themselves and others based on love, even though they do not know how to receive love. This puts people in a vulnerable position, always feeling judged for not having enough love, or finding themselves accusing others of not having love. And eventually, they discover that everything they dreamed about is falling apart.

Vertical and Horizontal Love

So let us look at where love originates and how this love eminates. I will say there are two kinds of love: one is vertical and the other is horizontal. Vertical love is the connection between humankind and God, who is the Origin of love. The second direction of love is horizontal. This is the love between two individuals, especially between man and woman, called conjugal love. Until we can receive the vertical love from God, it is an illusion to believe there can be real love between human beings, regardless many actions have a semblance of belonging to the realm of love.

Until human beings can accept to acknowledge the Origin of love, we can only dream about love or sing about love. Recognizing the Origin of love is the beginning of being able to receive love. Nowadays, many people like to believe they are themselves some kind of origin, especially since they can create and transform so many material things. If human beings believe they are the origin of love, then I can understand why they would don't feel they need to turn to God for love. But surely this would be a major mistake.

The reality is that God is the only being who possesses true love. Without receiving His love, you cannot give love to other people who live with you or who you meet in your life. To begin to receive His love, you need to learn to be grateful about what God created for humanity and of course, for the everyday gifts in your life. Maybe it can appear to be difficult to have this awareness of gratefulness all the time, but regardless of that, it is the most important thing you can do for your own life, as well as for any person who has the chance to approach you during your life's journey. Without this gratefulness toward God or heaven, you cannot receive the love that is necessary for you to love your friends, your spouse, and even your own child.

Secondly, you need to learn horizontal gratefulness, which is the gratefulness toward what people give to you. A grateful mind will create and maintain a close relationship between you and your partner, you and your children, or you and any other person, because love will be free to circulate in your midst.

By accepting to express gratitude to God for everything that is living around you, you will find that God will respond to you by giving all of His love, if you can take all of it. I believe God will be very excited to see someone who, for the first time, responds to the love He gives through all things. Also, your child will be super happy to know he is born from someone who receives the love of God. This child will not have a problem to respond gratefully to the person who produced him, in both the short term as well as for eternity. Indeed, any person who learns to be grateful about what was created around his or her life will surely be a person that others will wish to be close to.

Gratitude Produces Humility

So, the more you accept to be grateful, the more you can become humble and full of love. The action of gratefulness toward God will transform your eyes, allowing you to see love all around you. As well, your mind will enlarge to the size corresponding to the amount of your gratefulness. Conversely, if you reject the action of being grateful, your mind will become more and more narrow, to a size where you can no longer perceive any goodness around you or within you.

Remember that only love can transform you. Without it you cannot function in harmony with each situation you come across. If you learn to be grateful to God, you will experience a new feeling inside yourself that will permit you to realize life is made in color, not in black and white, and because of that you will not want to destroy any aspect of life. This is the gift of God's love inside your soul.

Without a fresh feeling every day, you will lose the desire to live with the same people over and over, to the point you can consider they are no longer interesting or attractive. It is not just because you had a good night's sleep that you feel the next day is a new, fresh day. It is only with true love from God that you can feel fresh or excited to live with the people around you. You may have heard people say that love makes us blind. Indeed, only love can allow us to continue to live with each other with enthusiasm every day. Usually after some time of living together, people lose interest in each other because there is nothing new to discover. But if you learn to be grateful, the flow of God's love will rush inside you and will give you the strength to see people again and again as if for the first time.

Sometimes people tell me that they are grateful for each other even though they don't believe in the existence of God, but this is pretty rare. People can achieve a certain level of relationship by using positive language and speaking with an eloquent and polite vocabulary, but if vocabulary were enough to make us beautiful beings, we surely would just need to study specific vocabulary words over and over. The facts tell us that regardless we are able to speak in a well-mannered way, this does not give us the security of believing we have the love we so much wish to have.

But if we begin to learn our lesson of believing in God and being grateful to Him, then whatever we do or say will contain nothing except love. However, if you want to share words of gratefulness with each human being who is close to you, then you need to begin by speaking gratefully to God first. When you speak to God with a grateful mind, you are learning to speak in a lovely way at the same time. Then when you turn to somebody, you will have the most exciting language to share with that person, who will consider you to be romantic.

In observing human beings, though, I realize most people have little knowledge about God's existence or God's viewpoint. Indeed, it is difficult to be grateful to some Creator you do not know, but the more you begin to appreciate God's creation, from the small to the big, the more God will trust you with His diamond, which is His heart of love.

Mastering Gratefulness

Please understand that if you do not recognize what God gives to you, He cannot lead you to discover His heart. Knowing we are like a container, we can understand that within our life we need to fill up our container with the love of God, to the point where we can resemble the heart of God, instead of just existing as a being with an empty soul. If we choose to be grateful until the last day of our physical life, our heart will become full of the love of God, and we will resemble the heart of God.

Until you fill up your container with love, you can only give your physical talents or mental talents to your family or to other people. Because every human being is fundamentally made as a being of love, if you cannot fulfill their need to receive love, your family and friends cannot fully respond to you as they wish.

Therefore, I would like you to become a master in learning and practicing gratefulness. For this, regardless you are educated to have positive thoughts or you believe it is good to turn to God, you also need to realize there is some rejection in yourself toward the realm of feelings that blocks you from learning to be grateful toward God. For example, when you want to say 'thank you' to somebody, it seems impossible to open your mouth. In your mind you are grateful but your body has some barrier to say it.

This is why it is not easy to express your mind of gratefulness. Many times you say to yourself that you need to say 'thank you' to your husband or wife for the beautiful smile he or she gives when you come home, but if you look at how many times you actually say 'thank you', you will be shocked to realize you didn't say it for maybe one whole year. In your mind you recognized his or her smile, yet your mouth didn't say what you saw as being good.

This is just one example from among millions. You even act like this in front of God. Maybe you believe you are grateful to God because in your mind you recognize what God gives to you, but you never verbalize to God what you receive. Or, if you do say something to God, you do not accurately recount the event. This is a profound problem. If you want to receive the love of God, just to think well does not guarantee that you will be able to receive that love. Only by speaking about the goodness you experienced, regardless of who created that goodness or where it came from, can the love of God descend to you, like a vacuum drawing in the air.

For example, imagine that a person whom you do not get along well with says something nice to you one day, and then after this surprising event, you decide to turn to God. However, instead of saying gratefully, "God, this person spoke nicely to me, what a miracle!" what you actually say is, "Do you know, God, this person was pretending to be nice to me today." Which report will allow God to melt? God loves to hear a true story that will make Him melt. Only if you speak gratefully according to what was truly happening will His love come to you to nourish your soul.

The Language of Love

When you want to make a positive effect on some person, you try to find some story that is connected to his or her life. If you can do this, that person will feel moved and happy and will want to respond to you. It is the same with God. If you speak about something that is connected to His life then God cannot help but love you. Not just any story can melt God's heart. The only language that God can hear is the language of gratefulness.

The more you learn to speak with gratitude, the more you will acquire the language of love. There are many different ways to do so. One way is to give the big picture first, and then slowly describe the details of that picture. This will gain the attention of any person listening to you. Similarly, when you speak to God, He will love the details of your story because He feels He can discover something that He did not know. When you start to be grateful you will realize there are many things around you about which you want to talk to God, especially if you begin to observe the details in addition to the big picture.

There are three levels of maturity and three levels of gratefulness corresponding to them. The first level is to recognize the physical creation that supports your body. The second level is to be grateful for the knowledge you receive and for all the education given to you to become the person you are. The third level is to be grateful for all the events that create happiness in you, or in other words, for love, which is connected to the realm of emotion. The moment you begin to recognize the realm of emotion inside yourself and gratefully tell God about it, the love of God can begin to be truly free within you.

These three levels represent the three aspects of yourself. Your body represents the physical matter of the creation. Your mind is invisible and represents knowledge and intellect. The third part of yourself is your heart, corresponding to your emotions, which resembles God. If you can recognize all three dimensions from now until the end of your physical life, and be grateful for them, I absolutely believe you will become a lovely human being, and will be recognized as a lovely being by the people around you.

So I hope you will choose to take the road of humility and gratitude. Do you understand now that loving God is to learn to be grateful to Him about your life? Loving each other means to be grateful about each other. If you lose gratefulness towards the beings you live with, you will lose love for them. Therefore, people will tell you that you do not love them.

You will also discover that there are some situations in life that make it difficult to be grateful, and due to this it is easy to take the opposite road, of negativity. The negative mind, or the mind of complaint, is actually 180 degrees opposite to the grateful mind. Through the action of complaining you reject any possibility of receiving love: its purpose is to make sure love cannot be with you or around you. Complaint has the property of destroying any sprouts that want to spring up in your soul. If you prevent all these sprouts from being born you will have a desert one day. I believe many human beings experience living in a desert because they judge every sprout that wants to lead them forward.

Create an Oasis Around You

Gratefulness wants life to grow bigger and wider, whereas complaint wants everything to get smaller and narrower. Look at your family, your city, or your nation and check what kind of attitude people have toward life. Do they complain or are they grateful? Our attitude toward our individual life will determine if we can receive the love that will nourish our souls. This truth is the same regarding the family level. A family will raise a beautiful child if the level of gratefulness within the family is amplified every day.

The same law can be applied to the city or the nation. If, for example, a nation can no longer find any reason to be grateful, it will become unstable and eventually it will be destroyed. Complaint is the disease that has the power to destroy the world. Throughout all the years you are on this planet Earth, you need to make a daily choice about which direction you want to go: the direction of self-destruction or the direction of growth. Your direction will either produce a desert or an oasis.

Without true love no one can become the being he or she was destined to become, or the person he or she wishes to be. Without the true love of God you are not capable of fulfilling any of your dreams, like becoming a good person, having a lovely spouse and a stable family, or having children who can respond to you with gratefulness on their part. All these dreams cannot be fulfilled if you cannot make yourself grateful enough so God can give His love to you.

The more you are grateful, the more you will also discover new levels of God's viewpoint. You will find that when you look at someone who is less fortunate, you will only have love for him or her. This will be a miracle in this time of history, when so many have lost their sensitivity toward others.

Young people usually start their lives with some level of positive mind, but as time passes they often lose it. Many start their marriage believing that their love will last a lifetime, yet after a few years they can no longer see anything positive in the person they once felt love for. The question is, where did the love go? The food you eat disappears into your molecules. Knowledge also disappears if it is not used. Is love also made in the same way as your molecules, having the potential to perish?

Yet for some reason, we believe love is made to live forever. Then why does love leave us, or why does it not increase in us, or between us and others? Until we can find a way to keep love in us, we are going to be miserable in this life and even more so after this life, because we will have not have acquired the nature of love that can help us to communicate with God and with others for eternity.

Fulfill Your Original Purpose

Unless we adopt the attitude of gratefulness, we will not be able to receive the knowledge from God that permits us to develop a love that welcomes everything existing. Instead we will develop a different mind that will make us consider that only a few things should be allowed to exist.

If we cannot become one with God, our original purpose cannot be fulfilled, and this is a very dramatic situation. However, as we expand our gratefulness, the love of God becomes more and more substantial within our heart, and we become more and more mature with age. This viewpoint is different from our usual viewpoint, where we believe just because our bodies become old we can consider ourselves to be mature. In reality, only when our love increases will the people around us be happy, particularly our spouse. I see too many human beings who carry nothing inside themselves, as well as human beings who carry anger or hatred in their soul, accusing each other because they cannot receive love from each other.

So I hope now you can understand what causes this lack of love. Instead of accusing each other or accepting emptiness as the way God created us, it is time to learn to be grateful so we can begin to receive the love that was around us from the day we were born, and which is our true destiny.

After all these words I hope you will be humble enough to accept whatever reality you find with gratitude, regardless it is in many cases a sad reality. But I trust you can now change it by learning to be grateful throughout any situation that arises in your life. Gratefulness has many effects, first in you, then in other people, and also in God. When you live your life with a deep sense of positivity, God feels He can, after all, give His heart to you. From God's viewpoint your new behavior is actually liberating His heart, because you give Him the possibility to give His love to you.

I hope you will take

what we have learned seriously. The main idea is that the more you are grateful, the more your mind will discover God's mind and become one with God's mind, to the point where God's feeling can pass through your heart. If you can do so, then you will always feel happy and never alone. By being grateful to God all your life you will feel an abundance of love for your spouse, your children, and all the people around you.

The key point in all of this is to discover the power of having a grateful mind. Please live well and with a humble heart. Please have the attitude of a child who discovers everything for the first time, and accepts everything as the most beautiful and wondrous thing that can happen to him or her.

Thank you. May True Love be with you.